# Banjo Paterson's
# BUSH BALLADS

# *Banjo Paterson's*

# BUSH BALLADS

VIKING
*an imprint of*
PENGUIN BOOKS

VIKING

Published by the Penguin Group
Penguin Group (Australia)
250 Camberwell Road, Camberwell, Victoria 3124, Australia
(a division of Pearson Australia Group Pty Ltd)
Penguin Group (USA) Inc.
375 Hudson Street, New York, New York 10014, USA
Penguin Group (Canada)
90 Eglinton Avenue East, Suite 700, Toronto, Canada ON M4P 2Y3
(a division of Pearson Penguin Canada Inc.)
Penguin Books Ltd
80 Strand, London WC2R 0RL England
Penguin Ireland
25 St Stephen's Green, Dublin 2, Ireland
(a division of Penguin Books Ltd)
Penguin Books India Pvt Ltd
11 Community Centre, Panchsheel Park, New Delhi – 110 017, India
Penguin Group (NZ)
67 Apollo Drive, Rosedale, North Shore 0632, New Zealand
(a division of Pearson New Zealand Ltd)
Penguin Books (South Africa) (Pty) Ltd
24 Sturdee Avenue, Rosebank, Johannesburg 2196, South Africa

Penguin Books Ltd, Registered Offices: 80 Strand, London, WC2R 0RL, England

First published by Penguin Group (Australia), 2007

3 5 7 9 10 8 6 4 2



Cover and text design by Karen Trump © Penguin Group (Australia)
Cover image from the Mitchell Library, State Library of New South Wales
Typeset in Palatino by Sunset Digital Pty Ltd, Brisbane, Queensland
Printed and bound in Australia by McPherson's Printing Group, Maryborough, Victoria

National Library of Australia
Cataloguing-in-Publication data:

Paterson, A. B. (Andrew Barton), 1864–1941.
Banjo Paterson's bush ballads.
ISBN 978 0 670 07092 3.
1. Ballads, English – Australia. I. Title.

A821.2

penguin.com.au

# Contents

Lost . . . . . . . . . . . . . . . . . . . . . . . . . . . 1
Uncle Bill. . . . . . . . . . . . . . . . . . . . . . . . . 3
How M'Ginnis Went Missing . . . . . . . . . . . 5
Clancy of the Overflow . . . . . . . . . . . . . . . 6
Gilhooley's Estate . . . . . . . . . . . . . . . . . . 10
The Man from Snowy River . . . . . . . . . . . 12
Those Names . . . . . . . . . . . . . . . . . . . . . 16
On Kiley's Run . . . . . . . . . . . . . . . . . . . . 17
Come-by-Chance . . . . . . . . . . . . . . . . . . 21
In the Droving Days . . . . . . . . . . . . . . . . 23
The Flying Gang. . . . . . . . . . . . . . . . . . . 26
A Mountain Station. . . . . . . . . . . . . . . . . 28
A Bushman's Song . . . . . . . . . . . . . . . . . 30
The Pannikin Poet. . . . . . . . . . . . . . . . . 32
In Defence of the Bush . . . . . . . . . . . . . . 34
An Answer to Various Bards. . . . . . . . . . . 38
A Bush Christening. . . . . . . . . . . . . . . . . 40
Black Swans . . . . . . . . . . . . . . . . . . . . . 42
How Gilbert Died . . . . . . . . . . . . . . . . . . 44
The Man Who Was Away . . . . . . . . . . . . . 47
Saltbush Bill. . . . . . . . . . . . . . . . . . . . . . 50
The Two Devines . . . . . . . . . . . . . . . . . . 53

The Daylight is Dying . . . . . . . . . . . . . . . 55

Jim Carew . . . . . . . . . . . . . . . . . . . . . 57

The Swagman's Rest . . . . . . . . . . . . . . . 59

The Wind's Message . . . . . . . . . . . . . . . 61

Under the Shadow of Kiley's Hill. . . . . . . . 64

Waltzing Matilda (Original Version) . . . . . . . . . 66

Waltzing Matilda (Popular Version) . . . . . . . . . 68

Brumby's Run . . . . . . . . . . . . . . . . . . 70

With the Cattle. . . . . . . . . . . . . . . . . . 72

Song of the Artesian Water. . . . . . . . . . . . 78

The Story of Mongrel Grey . . . . . . . . . . . . 80

Pioneers . . . . . . . . . . . . . . . . . . . . . 83

By the Grey Gulf-Water . . . . . . . . . . . . . 86

Saltbush Bill's Second Fight . . . . . . . . . . 88

It's Grand . . . . . . . . . . . . . . . . . . . . 93

The Old Australian Ways . . . . . . . . . . . . 95

The Road to Gundagai . . . . . . . . . . . . . . 100

Santa Claus in the Bush . . . . . . . . . . . . . 102

Sunrise on the Coast . . . . . . . . . . . . . . 106

Song of the Wheat. . . . . . . . . . . . . . . . 107

The Mountain Squatter . . . . . . . . . . . . . 109

The Gundaroo Bullock. . . . . . . . . . . . . . 112

List of photographs . . . . . . . . . . . . . . . 114

# Lost

'He ought to be home,' said the old man, 'without there's something amiss.
He only went to the Two-mile – he ought to be back by this.
He *would* ride the Reckless filly, he *would* have his wilful way;
And, here, he's not back at sundown – and what will his mother say?

'He was always his mother's idol, since ever his father died;
And there isn't a horse on the station that he isn't game to ride.
But that Reckless mare is vicious, and if once she gets away
He hasn't got strength to hold her – and what will his mother say?'

The old man walked to the sliprail, and peered up the dark'ning track,
And looked and longed for the rider that would never more come back;
And the mother came and clutched him, with sudden, spasmodic fright:
'What has become of my Willie? Why isn't he home tonight?'

Away in the gloomy ranges, at the foot of an ironbark,
The bonnie, winsome laddie was lying stiff and stark;
For the Reckless mare had smashed him against a leaning limb,
And his comely face was battered, and his merry eyes were dim.

And the thoroughbred chestnut filly, the saddle beneath her flanks,
Was away like fire through the ranges to join the wild mob's ranks;
And a broken-hearted woman and an old man worn and grey
Were searching all night in the ranges till sunrise brought the day.

And the mother kept feebly calling, with a hope that would not die,
'Willie! where are you, Willie?' But how can the dead reply;
And hope died out with the daylight, and the darkness brought despair,
God pity the stricken mother, and answer the widow's prayer!

Though far and wide they sought him, they found not where he fell;
For the ranges held him precious, and guarded their treasure well.
The wattle blooms above him, and the bluebells blow close by,
And the brown bees buzz the secret, and the wild birds sing reply.

But the mother pined and faded, and cried, and took no rest,
And rode each day to the ranges on her hopeless, weary quest.
Seeking her loved one ever, she faded and pined away,
But with strength of her great affection she still sought very day.

'I know that sooner or later I shall find my boy,' she said.
But she came not home one evening, and they found her lying dead.
And stamped on the poor pale features, as the spirit homeward pass'd,
Was an angel smile of gladness – she had found the boy at last.

*(1887)*

## *Uncle Bill*

My Uncle Bill! My Uncle Bill!
How doth my heart with anguish thrill!
For he, our chief, our Robin Hood,
Has gone to jail for stealing wood!
With tears and sobs my voice I raise
To celebrate my uncle's praise;
With all my strength, with all my skill,
I'll sing the song of Uncle Bill.

Convivial to the last degree,
An open-hearted sportsman he.
Did midnight howls our slumbers rob,
We said, 'It's uncle "on the job".'
When sounds of fight rang sharply out,
Then Bill was bound to be about,
The foremost figure in 'the scrap',
A terror to the local 'trap'.
To drink, or fight, or maim, or kill,
Came all alike to Uncle Bill.
And when he faced the music's squeak
At Central Court before the beak,
How carefully we sought our fob
To pay his fine of forty bob!
Recall the happy days of yore
When Uncle Bill went forth to war!
When all the street with strife was filled
And both the traps got nearly killed.
When the lone cabman on the stand
Was 'stoushed' by Bill's unaided hand,
And William mounted, filled with rum,
And drove the cab to kingdom come.
Remember, too, that famous fray
When the 'Black-reds', who hold their sway
O'er Surry Hills and Shepherd's Bush,
Descended on the 'Liver Push'.

Who cheered both parties long and loud?
Who heaved blue metal at the crowd!
And sooled his bulldog, Fighting Bet,
To bite, haphazard, all she met?
And when the mob were lodged in gaol
Who telegraphed to me for bail?
And – here I think he showed his sense –
Who calmly turned Queen's evidence?
Enough! I now must end my song,
My needless anguish, why prolong?
From what I've said, you'll own, I'm sure,
That Uncle Bill was pretty 'pure',
So, rowdies all, your glasses fill,
And – drink it standing – 'Uncle Bill'.

*(1888)*

# How M'Ginnis Went Missing

Let us cease our idle chatter,
  Let the tears bedew our cheek,
For a man from Tallangatta
  Has been missing for a week.

Where the roaring, flooded Murray
  Covered all the lower land,
There he started in a hurry,
  With a bottle in his hand.

And his fate is hid for ever,
  But the public seem to think
That he slumbered by the river,
  'Neath the influence of drink.

And they scarcely seem to wonder
  That the river, wide and deep,
Never woke him with its thunder,
  Never stirred him in his sleep.

As the crushing logs came sweeping,
  And their tumult filled the air,
Then M'Ginnis murmured, sleeping,
  ''Tis a wake in ould Kildare.'

So the river rose and found him
  Sleeping softly by the stream,
And the cruel waters drowned him
  Ere he wakened from his dream.

And the blossom-tufted wattle,
  Blooming brightly on the lea
Saw M'Ginnis and the bottle
  Going drifting out to sea.

*(1889)*

## *Clancy of the Overflow*

I had written him a letter which I had, for want of better
  Knowledge, sent to where I met him down the Lachlan, years ago,
He was shearing when I knew him, so I sent the letter to him,
  Just 'on spec', addressed as follows: 'Clancy, of the Overflow'.

And an answer came directed in a writing unexpected,
  (And I think the same was written with a thumbnail dipped in tar)
'Twas his shearing mate who wrote it, and *verbatim* I will quote it:
  'Clancy's gone to Queensland droving, and we don't know where he are.'

In my wild erratic fancy visions come to me of Clancy
  Gone a-droving 'down the Cooper' where the western drovers go;
As the stock are slowly stringing, Clancy rides behind them singing,
  For the drover's life has pleasures that the townsfolk never know.

And the bush hath friends to meet him, and their kindly voices greet him
  In the murmur of the breezes and the river on its bars,
And he sees the vision splendid of the sunlit plains extended,
  And at night the wondrous glory of the everlasting stars.

I am sitting in my dingy little office, where a stingy
  Ray of sunlight struggles feebly down between the houses tall,
And the foetid air and gritty of the dusty, dirty city
  Through the open window floating, spreads its foulness over all.

And in the place of lowing cattle, I can hear the fiendish rattle
  Of the tramways and the buses making hurry down the street,
And the language uninviting of the gutter children fighting,
  Comes fitfully and faintly through the ceaseless tramp of feet.

And the hurrying people daunt me, and their pallid faces haunt me
  As they shoulder one another in their rush and nervous haste,
With their eager eyes and greedy, and their stunted forms and weedy,
  For townsfolk have not time to grow, they have no time to waste.

And I somehow rather fancy that I'd like to change with Clancy,
  Like to take a turn at droving where the seasons come and go,
While he faced the round eternal of the cashbook and the journal –
  But I doubt he'd suit the office, Clancy, of 'The Overflow'.

*(1889)*

# *Gilhooley's Estate*

*A ballad concerning the amalgamation of the legal profession*

Oh, Mr Gilhooley he turned up his toes,
As most of us do, soon or late;
And Jones was a lawyer, as everyone knows,
So they took him Gilhooley's estate.

Gilhooley in life had been living so free
'Twas thought his possessions were great,
So Jones, with a smile, says, 'There's many a fee
For me in Gilhooley's estate.'

They made out a list of his property fine,
It totalled a thousand and eight;
But the debts were nine hundred and ninety and nine –
The debts of Gilhooley's estate.

So Mrs Gilhooley says, 'Jones, my dear man,
My childer have little to ait:
Just keep the expenses as low as you can
Against poor Gilhooley's estate.'

But Jones says, 'The will isn't clear in its terms,
I fear it will need some debate,
And the law won't allow me (attorneys are worms)
To appear in Gilhooley's estate.'

So a barrister man, with a wig on his head,
And a brief in his hand quite elate,
Went up to the Court where they bury the dead,
Just to move in Gilhooley's estate.

But His Honour the Judge said, 'I think that the joint
Legatees must be called to pro*bate* –
*Ex parte* Pokehorney is clear on the point –
The point of Gilhooley's estate.

'I order a suit to be bought just to try
If this is correct that I state –
A nice friendly suit, and the costs, by and by,
Must be borne by Gilhooley's estate.'

So Mrs Gilhooley says, 'Jones, you'll appear!
Thim barristers' fees is too great;
The suit is but friendly.' 'Attorneys, my dear,
Can't be heard in Gilhooley's estate.'

From Barristers' Court there's a mighty hurrah
Arises both early and late;
It's only the whoop of the Junior Bar
Dividing Gilhooley's estate.

*(1890)*

# The Man from Snowy River

There was movement at the station, for the word had passed around
That the colt from old Regret had got away,
And had joined the wild bush horses – he was worth a thousand pound,
So all the cracks had gathered to the fray.
All the tried and noted riders from the stations near and far
Had mustered at the homestead overnight,
For the bushmen love hard riding where the wild bush horses are,
And the stockhorse snuffs the battle with delight.

There was Harrison, who made his pile when Pardon won the cup,
The old man with his hair as white as snow;
But few could ride beside him when his blood was fairly up –
He would go wherever horse and man could go.
And Clancy of the Overflow came down to lend a hand,
No better horseman ever held the reins;
For never horse could throw him while the saddle-girths would stand,
He learnt to ride while droving on the plains.

And one was there, a stripling on a small and weedy beast,
He was something like a racehorse undersized,
With a touch of Timor pony – three parts thoroughbred at least –
And such as are by mountain horsemen prized.
He was hard and tough and wiry – just the sort that won't say die –
There was courage in his quick impatient tread;
And he bore the badge of gameness in his quick and fiery eye,
And the proud and lofty carriage of his head.

But still so slight and weedy, one would doubt his power to stay,
And the old man said, 'That horse will never do
For a long and tiring gallop – lad, you'd better stop away,
These hills are far too rough for such as you.'
So he waited sad and wistful – only Clancy stood his friend –
'I think we ought to let him come,' he said;
'I warrant he'll be with us when he's wanted at the end,
For both his horse and he are mountain bred.

'He hails from Snowy River, up by Kosciusko's side,
Where the hills are twice as steep and twice as rough,
Where a horse's hoofs strike firelight from the flint stones every stride,
The man that holds his own is good enough.
And the Snowy River riders on the mountains make their home,
Where the river runs those giant hills between;
I have seen full many horsemen since I first commenced to roam,
But nowhere yet such horsemen have I seen.'

So he went – they found the horses by the big mimosa clump –
They raced away towards the mountain's brow,
And the old man gave his orders, 'Boys, go at them from the jump,
No use to try for fancy riding now.
And, Clancy, you must wheel them, try and wheel them to the right.
Ride boldly, lad, and never fear the spills,
For never yet was rider that could keep the mob in sight,
If once they gain the shelter of those hills.'

So Clancy rode to wheel them – he was racing on the wing
Where the best and boldest riders take their place,
And he raced his stockhorse past them, and he made the ranges ring
With the stockwhip, as he met them face to face.
Then they halted for a moment, while he swung the dreaded lash,
But they saw their well-loved mountain full in view,
And they charged beneath the stockwhip with a sharp and sudden dash,
And off into the mountain scrub they flew.

Then fast the horsemen followed, where the gorges deep and black
Resounded to the thunder of their tread,
And the stockwhips woke the echoes, and they fiercely answered back
From cliffs and crags that beetled overhead.
And upward, ever upward, the wild horses held their way,
Where mountain ash and kurrajong grew wide;
And the old man muttered fiercely, 'We may bid the mob good day,
*No* man can hold them down the other side.'

When they reached the mountain's summit, even Clancy took a pull,
It well might make the boldest hold their breath,
The wild hop scrub grew thickly, and the hidden ground was full
Of wombat holes, and any slip was death.
But the man from Snowy River let the pony have his head,
And he swung his stockwhip round and gave a cheer,
And he raced him down the mountain like a torrent down its bed,
While the others stood and watched in very fear.

He sent the flint stones flying, but the pony kept his feet,
He cleared the fallen timber in his stride,
And the man from Snowy River never shifted in his seat –
It was grand to see that mountain horseman ride.
Through the stringybarks and saplings, on the rough and broken ground,
Down the hillside at a racing pace he went;
And he never drew the bridle till he landed safe and sound,
At the bottom of that terrible descent.

He was right among the horses as they climbed the further hill,
And the watchers on the mountain standing mute,
Saw him ply the stockwhip fiercely, he was right among them still,
As he raced across the clearing in pursuit.
Then they lost him for a moment, where two mountain gullies met
In the ranges, but a final glimpse reveals
On a dim and distant hillside the wild horses racing yet,
With the man from Snowy River at their heels.

And he ran them single-handed till their sides were white with foam.
He followed like a bloodhound on their track,
Till they halted, cowed and beaten, then he turned their heads for home,
And alone and unassisted brought them back.
But his hardy mountain pony he could scarcely raise a trot,
He was blood from hip to shoulder from the spur;
But his pluck was still undaunted, and his courage fiery hot,
For never yet was mountain horse a cur.

And down by Kosciusko, where the pine-clad ridges raise
Their torn and rugged battlements on high,
Where the air is clear as crystal, and the white stars fairly blaze
At midnight in the cold and frosty sky,
And where around The Overflow the reed beds sweep and sway
To the breezes, and the rolling plains are wide,
The Man from Snowy River is a household word today,
And the stockmen tell the story of his ride.

*(1890)*

## *Those Names*

The Shearers sat in the firelight, hearty and hale and strong,
After the hard day's shearing, passing the joke along:
The 'ringer' that shore a hundred, as they never were shorn before,
And the novice who, toiling bravely, had tommyhawked half a score,
The tar boy, the cook, and the slushy, the sweeper that swept the board,
The picker-up, and the penner, with the rest of the shearing horde.
There were men from the inland stations where the skies like a furnace glow,
And men from the Snowy River, the land of the frozen snow;
There were swarthy Queensland drovers who reckoned all land by miles,
And farmers' sons from the Murray, where many a vineyard smiles.
They started at telling stories when they wearied of cards and games,
And to give these stories a flavour they threw in some local names,
And a man from the bleak Monaro, away on the tableland,
He fixed his eyes on the ceiling, and he started to play his hand.

He told them of Adjintoothbong, where the pine-clad mountains freeze,
And the weight of the snow in summer breaks branches off the trees,
And, as he warmed to the business, he let them have it strong –
Nimitybelle, Conargo, Wheeo, Bongongolong;
He lingered over them fondly, because they recalled to mind
A thought of the old bush homestead, and the girl that he left behind.
Then the shearers all sat silent till a man in the corner rose;
Said he, 'I've travelled aplenty but never heard names like those,
Out in the western districts, out on the Castlereagh
Most of the names are easy – short for a man to say.
'You've heard of Mungrybambone and the Gundabluey pine,
Quobbotha, Girilambone, and Terramungamine,
Quambone, Eunonyhareenha, Wee Waa, and Buntijo –'
But the rest of the shearers stopped him, 'For the sake of your jaw, go slow,
If you reckon those names are short ones out where such names prevail,
Just try and remember some long ones before you begin the tale.'

And the man from the western district, though never a word he said,
Just winked with his dexter eyelid, and then he retired to bed.

*(1890)*

## *On Kiley's Run*

The roving breezes come and go
  On Kiley's Run,
The sleepy river murmurs low,
And far away one dimly sees
Beyond the stretch of forest trees –
Beyond the foothills dusk and dun –
The ranges sleeping in the sun
  On Kiley's Run.

'Tis many years since first I came
  To Kiley's Run,
More years than I would care to name
Since I, a stripling, used to ride
For miles and miles at Kiley's side,
The while in stirring tones he told
The stories of the days of old
  On Kiley's Run.

I see the old bush homestead now
  On Kiley's Run,
Just nestled down beneath the brow
Of one small ridge above the sweep
Of river flat, where willows weep
And jasmine flowers and roses bloom,
The air was laden with perfume
  On Kiley's Run.

We lived the good old station life
  On Kiley's Run,
With little thought of care or strife.
Old Kiley seldom used to roam,
He liked to make the Run his home,
The swagman never turned away
With empty hand at close of day
  From Kiley's Run.

We kept a racehorse now and then
  On Kiley's Run,
And neighb'ring stations brought their men
To meetings where the sport was free,
And dainty ladies came to see
Their champions ride; with laugh and song
The old house rang the whole night long
  On Kiley's Run.

The station hands were friends I wot
  On Kiley's Run,
A reckless, merry-hearted lot –
All splendid riders, and they knew
The 'boss' was kindness through and through.
Old Kiley always stood their friend,
And so they served him to the end
  On Kiley's Run.

But droughts and losses came apace
  To Kiley's Run,
Till ruin stared him in the face;
He toiled and toiled while lived the light,
He dreamed of overdrafts at night:
At length, because he could not pay,
His bankers took the stock away
  From 'Kiley's Run'.

Old Kiley stood and saw them go
  From Kiley's Run.
The well-bred cattle marching slow;
His stockmen, mates for many a day,
They wrung his hand and went away.
Too old to make another start,
Old Kiley died – of broken heart,
  On Kiley's Run.

The owner lives in England now
  Of Kiley's Run.
He knows a racehorse from a cow;
But that is all he knows of stock:
His chiefest care is how to dock
Expenses, and he sends from town
To cut the shearers' wages down
  On Kiley's Run.

There are no neighbours anywhere
  Near Kiley's Run.
The hospitable homes are bare,
The gardens gone; for no pretence
Must hinder cutting down expense:
The homestead that we held so dear
Contains a half-paid overseer
  On Kiley's Run.

All life and sport and hope have died
  On Kiley's Run.
No longer there the stockmen ride;
For sour-faced boundary riders creep
On mongrel horses after sheep,
Through ranges where, at racing speed,
Old Kiley used to 'wheel the lead'
  On Kiley's Run.

There runs a lane for thirty miles
  Through Kiley's Run.
On either side the herbage smiles,
But wretched trav'lling sheep must pass
Without a drink or blade of grass
Thro' that long lane of death and shame:
The weary drovers curse the name
  Of Kiley's Run.

The name itself is changed of late
  Of Kiley's Run.
They call it 'Chandos Park Estate'.
The lonely swagman through the dark
Must hump his swag past Chandos Park.
The name is English, don't you see,
The old name sweeter sounds to me
  Of 'Kiley's Run'.

I cannot guess what fate will bring
  To Kiley's Run –
For chances come and changes ring –
I scarcely think 'twill always be
Locked up to suit an absentee;
And if he lets it out in farms
His tenants soon will carry arms
  On Kiley's Run.

*(1890)*

# *Come-by-Chance*

As I pondered very weary o'er a volume long and dreary –
For the plot was void of interest – 'twas that Postal Guide, in fact,
There I learnt the true location, distance, size, and population
Of each township, town, and village in the radius of the Act.

And I learnt that Puckawidgee stands beside the Murrumbidgee,
And that Booleroi and Bumble get their letters twice a year,
Also that the post inspector, when he visited Collector,
Closed the office up instanter, and re-opened Dungalear.

But my languid mood forsook me, when I found a name that took me,
Quite by chance I came across it – 'Come-by-Chance' was what I read;
No location was assigned it, not a thing to help one find it,
Just an 'N' which stood for northward, and the rest was all unsaid.

I shall leave my home, and forthward wander stoutly to the northward
Till I come by chance across it, and I'll straightaway settle down,
For there can't be any hurry, nor the slightest cause for worry
Where the telegraph don't reach you nor the railways run to town.

And one's letters and exchanges come by chance across the ranges,
Where a wiry young Australian leads a pack horse once a week,
And the good news grows by keeping, and you're spared the pain
of weeping
Over bad news when the mailman drops the letters in the creek.

But I fear, and more's the pity, that there's really no such city,
For there's not a man can find it of the shrewdest folk I know,
'Come-by-Chance', be sure it never means a land of fierce endeavour,
It is just the careless country where the dreamers only go.

Though we work and toil and hustle in our life of haste and bustle,
All that makes our life worth living comes unstriven for and free;
Man may weary and importune, but the fickle goddess Fortune
Deals him out his pain or pleasure careless what his worth may be.

All the happy times entrancing, days of sport and nights of dancing,
Moonlit rides and stolen kisses, pouting lips and loving glance:
When you think of these be certain you have looked behind the curtain,
You have had the luck to linger just a while in 'Come-by-Chance'.

*(1891)*

# In the Droving Days

'Only a pound,' said the auctioneer,
'Only a pound; and I'm standing here
Selling this animal, gain or loss.
Only a pound for the drover's horse;
One of the sort that was ne'er afraid,
One of the boys of the Old Brigade;
Thoroughly honest and game, I'll swear,
Only a little the worse for wear;
Plenty as bad to be seen in town,
Give me a bid and I'll knock him down;
Sold as he stands, and without recourse,
Give me a bid for the drover's horse.'

Loitering there in an aimless way
Somehow I noticed the poor old grey,
Weary and battered and screwed, of course,
Yet when I noticed the old grey horse,
The rough bush saddle, and single rein
Of the bridle laid on his tangled mane,
Straightaway the crowd and the auctioneer
Seemed on a sudden to disappear,
Melted away in a kind of haze,
For my heart went back to the droving days.

Back to the road, and I crossed again
Over the miles of the saltbush plain –
The shining plain that is said to be
The dried-up bed of an inland sea,
Where the air so dry and so clear and bright
Refracts the sun with a wondrous light,
And out in the dim horizon makes
The deep blue gleam of the phantom lakes.

At dawn of the day we would feel the breeze
That stirred the boughs of the sleeping trees,
And brought a breath of the fragrance rare
That comes and goes in that scented air;
For the trees and grass and the shrubs contain
A dry sweet scent on the saltbush plain.
For those that love it and understand,
The saltbush plain is a wonderland.
A wondrous country, where nature's ways
Were revealed to me in the droving days.

We saw the fleet wild horses pass,
And the kangaroos through the Mitchell grass,
The emu ran with her frightened brood
All unmolested and unpursued.
But there rose a shout and a wild hubbub
When the dingo raced for his native scrub,
And he paid right dear for his stolen meals
With the drovers' dogs at his wretched heels.
For we ran him down at a rattling pace,
While the pack horse joined in the stirring chase.
And a wild halloo at the kill we'd raise –
We were light of heart in the droving days.

'Twas a drover's horse, and my hand again
Made a move to close on a fancied rein.
For I felt the swing and the easy stride
Of the grand old horse that I use to ride
In drought or plenty, in good or ill,
That same old steed was my comrade still;
The old grey horse with his honest ways
Was a mate to me in the droving days.

When we kept our watch in the cold and damp,
If the cattle broke from the sleeping camp,
Over the flats and across the plain,
With my head bent down on his waving mane,
Through the boughs above and the stumps below
On the darkest night I would let him go
At a racing speed; he would choose his course,
And my life was safe with the old grey horse.
But man and horse had a favourite job,
When an outlaw broke from a station mob,
With a right good will was the stockwhip plied,
As the old horse raced at the straggler's side,
And the greenhide whip such a weal would raise,
We could use the whip in the droving days.

'Only a pound!' and this was the end –
Only a pound for the drover's friend.
The drover's friend that had seen his day,
And now was worthless, and cast away
With a broken knee and a broken heart
To be flogged and starved in a hawker's cart.
Well, I made a bid for a sense of shame
And the memories dear of the good old game.

'Thank you? Guinea! and cheap at that!
Against you there in the curly hat!
Only a guinea, and one more chance,
Down he goes if there's no advance,
Third, and the last time, one! two! three!'
And the old grey horse was knocked down to me.
And now he's wandering, fat and sleek,
On the lucerne flats by the Homestead Creek;
I dare not ride him for fear he'd fall,
But he does a journey to beat them all,
For though he scarcely a trot can raise,
He can take me back to the droving days.

*(1891)*

# The Flying Gang

*A Railroad Song*

I served my time, in the days gone by,
In the railway's clash and clang,
And I worked my way to the end, and I
Was the head of the 'Flying Gang'.
'Twas a chosen band that was kept at hand
In case of an urgent need,
Was it south or north we were started forth
And away at our utmost speed.
If word reached town that a bridge was down,
The imperious summons rang –
'Come out with the pilot engine sharp,
And away with the flying gang.'

Then a piercing scream and a rush of steam
As the engine moved ahead,
With a measured beat by the slum and street
Of the busy town we fled,
By the uplands bright and the homesteads white,
With the rush of the western gale,
And the pilot swayed with the pace we made
As she rocked on the ringing rail.
And the country children clapped their hands
As the engine's echoes rang,
But their elders said, 'There is work ahead
When they send for the flying gang.'

Then across the miles of the saltbush plain
That gleamed with the morning dew,
Where the grasses waved like the ripening grain
The pilot engine flew,
A fiery rush in the open bush
Where the grade marks seemed to fly,
And the order sped on the wires ahead,
The pilot *must* go by.
The Governor's special must stand aside,
And the fast express go hang,
Let your orders be that the line is free
For the boys of the flying gang.

*(1891)*

# A Mountain Station

I bought a run a while ago,
  On country rough and ridgy,
Where wallaroos and wombats grow –
  The Upper Murrumbidgee.
The grass is rather scant, it's true,
  But this a fair exchange is,
The sheep can see a lovely view
  By climbing up the ranges.

And 'She-oak Flat''s the station's name,
  I'm not surprised at that, sirs:
The oaks were there before I came,
  And I supplied the flat, sirs.
A man would wonder how it's done,
  The stock so soon decreases –
They sometimes tumble off the run
  And break themselves to pieces.

I've tried to make expenses meet,
  But wasted all my labours,
The sheep the dingoes didn't eat
  Were stolen by the neighbours.
They stole my pears – my native pears –
  Those thrice-convicted felons,
And ravished from me unawares
  My crop of paddymelons.

And sometimes under sunny skies,
  Without an explanation,
The Murrumbidgee used to rise
  And overflow the station.
But this was caused (as now I know)
  When summer sunshine glowing
Had melted all Kiandra's snow
  And set the river going.

And in the news, perhaps you read:
  'Stock passings. Puckawidgee,
Fat cattle: Seven hundred head
  Swept down the Murrumbidgee;
Their destination's quite obscure,
  But, somehow, there's a notion,
Unless the river falls, they're sure
  To reach the Southern Ocean.'

So after that I'll give it best;
  No more with Fate I'll battle.
I'll let the river take the rest,
  For those were all my cattle.
And with one comprehensive curse
  I close my brief narration,
And advertise it in my verse –
  'For Sale! A Mountain Station'.

*(1891)*

# A Bushman's Song

I'm travellin' down the Castlereagh, and I'm a station hand,
I'm handy with the ropin' pole, I'm handy with the brand,
And I can ride a rowdy colt, or swing the axe all day,
But there's no demand for a station hand along the Castlereagh.

So it's shift, boys, shift, for there isn't the slightest doubt
That we've got to make a shift to the stations further out
With the packhorse runnin' after, for he follows like a dog,
We must strike across the country at the old jig-jog.

This old black horse I'm riding – if you'll notice what's his brand,
He wears the crooked R, you see – none better in the land.
He takes a lot of beatin', and the other day we tried,
For a bit of a joke, with a racing bloke, for twenty pounds aside.

It was shift, boys, shift, for there wasn't the slightest doubt,
That I had to make him shift, for the money was nearly out;
But he cantered home a winner, with the other one at the flog –
He's a red-hot sort of pick up with his old jig-jog.

I asked a cove for shearin' once along the Marthaguy:
'We shear non-union, here,' says he. 'I call it scab,' says I.
I looked along the shearin' floor before I turned to go –
There were eight or ten dashed Chinamen a-shearin' in a row.

It was shift, boys, shift, for there wasn't the slightest doubt
It was time to make a shift with the leprosy about.
So I saddled up my horses, and I whistled to my dog,
And I left his scabby station at the old jig-jog.

I went to Illawarra where my brother's got a farm,
He has to ask his landlord's leave before he lifts his arm;
The landlord owns the countryside – man, woman, dog, and cat,
They haven't the cheek to dare to speak without they touch
their hat.

It was shift, boys, shift, for there wasn't the slightest doubt
Their little landlord god and I would soon have fallen out;
Was I to touch my hat to him? – was I his bloomin' dog?
So I makes for up the country at the old jig-jog.

But it's time that I was movin', I've a mighty way to go
Till I drink artesian water from a thousand feet below;
Till I meet the overlanders with the cattle comin' down,
And I'll work a while till I make a pile, then have a spree in town.

So, it's shift, boys, shift, for there isn't the slightest doubt
We've got to make a shift to the stations further out;
The packhorse runs behind us, for he follows like a dog,
And we cross a lot of country at the old jig-jog.

*(1892)*

# The Pannikin Poet

There's nothing here sublime,
But just a roving rhyme,
Run off to pass the time,
  With nought titanic in
The theme that it supports
And, though it treats of quarts,
It's bare of golden thoughts –
  It's just a pannikin.

I think it's rather hard
That each Australian bard –
Each wan, poetic card –
  With thoughts galvanic in
His fiery soul alight,
In wild aerial flight,
Will sit him down and write
  About a pannikin.

He makes some new chum fare
From out his English lair
To hunt the native bear,
  That curious mannikin;
And then when times get bad
That wand'ring English lad
Writes out a message sad
  Upon his pannikin:

'Oh, mother, think of me
Beneath the wattle tree.'
(For you may bet that he
  Will drag the wattle in.)
'Oh, mother, here I think
That I shall have to sink
There ain't a single drink
  The water bottle in.'

The dingo homeward hies,
The sooty crows uprise
And caw their fierce surprise
  A tone Satanic in;
And bearded bushman tread
Around the sleeper's head –
'See here – the bloke is dead.'
  'Now, where's his pannikin?'

They read his words and weep,
And lay him down to sleep
Where wattle branches sweep
  A style mechanic in;
And, reader, that's the way
The poets of today
Spin out their little lay
  About a pannikin.

*(1892)*

# *In Defence of the Bush*

So you're back from up the country, Mister Lawson, where you went,
And you're cursing all the business in a bitter discontent;
Well, we grieve to disappoint you, and it makes us sad to hear
That it wasn't cool and shady – and there wasn't plenty beer,
And the loony bullock snorted when you first came into view;
Well, you know it's not often that he sees a swell like you;
And the roads were hot and dusty, and the plains were burnt and brown,
And no doubt you're better suited drinking lemon squash in town.

Yet, perchance, if you should journey down the very track you went
In a month or two at furthest you would wonder what it meant,
Where the sunbaked earth was gasping like a creature in its pain
You would find the grasses waving like a field of summer grain,
And the miles of thirsty gutters blocked with sand and choked
with mud,
You would find them mighty rivers with a turbid, sweeping flood;
For the rain and drought and sunshine make no changes in the street,
In the sullen line of buildings and the ceaseless tramp of feet;
But the bush hath no moods and changes, as the seasons rise and fall,
And the men who know the bush land – they are loyal through it all.

But you found the bush was dismal and a land of no delight,
Did you chance to hear a chorus in the shearers' huts at night?
Did they 'rise up, William Riley' by the camp-fire's cheery blaze?
Did they rise him as we rose him in the good old droving days?
And the women of the homesteads and the men you chanced to meet –
Were their faces sour and saddened like the 'faces in the street',
And the 'shy selector children' – were they better now or worse
Than the little city urchins who would greet you with a curse?
Is not such a life much better than the squalid street and square
Where the fallen women flaunt it in the fierce electric glare,
Where the semptress plies her sewing till her eyes are sore and red
In a filthy, dirty attic toiling on for daily bread?
Did you hear no sweeter voices in the music of the bush
Than the roar of trams and buses, and the war whoop of 'the push'?

Did the magpies rouse your slumbers with their carol sweet and strange?
Did you hear the silver chiming of the bellbirds on the range?
But, perchance, the wild birds' music by your senses was despised,
For you say you'll stay in townships till the bush is civilised.
Would you make it a tea garden and on Sundays have a band
Where the 'blokes' might take their 'donahs', with a 'public' close at hand?
You had better stick to Sydney and make merry with the 'push',
For the bush will never suit you, and you'll never suit the bush.

*(1892)*

## An Answer to Various Bards

Well, I've waited mighty patient while they all came rolling in,
Mister Lawson, Mister Dyson, and the others of their kin,
With their dreadful, dismal stories of the overlander's camp,
How his fire is always smoky, and his boots are always damp;
And they paint it so terrific it would fill one's soul with gloom,
But you know they're fond of writing about 'corpses' and 'the tomb'
So, before they curse the bushland they should let their fancy range,
And take something for their livers, and be cheerful for a change.

Now, for instance, Mister Lawson – well, of course, we almost cried
At the sorrowful description how his 'little 'Arvie' died.
And we wept in silent sorrow when 'His Father's Mate' was slain;
Then he went and killed the father, and we had to weep again.
Ben Duggan and Jack Denver, too, he caused them to expire,
And he went and cooked the gander of Jack Dunn, of Nevertire;
And he spoke in terms prophetic of a revolution's beat,
When the world should hear the clamour of those people in the street;
But the shearer chaps who start it – why, he rounds on them in blame,
And he calls 'em 'agitators' who are living on the game.
So, no doubt, the bush is wretched if you judge it by the groan
Of the sad and soulful poet with a graveyard of his own.

But I 'over-write' the bushmen! Well, I own without a doubt
That I always see a hero in the 'man from furthest out'.
I could never contemplate him through an atmosphere of gloom,
And a bushman never struck me as a subject for 'the tomb'
If it ain't all 'golden sunshine' where the 'wattle branches wave',
Well, it ain't all damp and dismal, and it ain't all 'lonely grave'.
And, of course, there's no denying that the bushman's life is rough,
But a man can easy stand it if he's built of sterling stuff;
Tho' it's seldom that the drover gets a bed of eiderdown,
Yet the man who's born a bushman, he gets mighty sick of town,
For he's jotting down the figures, and he's adding up the bills
While his heart is simply aching for a sight of southern hills.
Then he hears a wool team passing with a rumble and a lurch,
Although the work is pressing yet it brings him off his perch.

For it stirs him like a message from his station friends afar
And he seems to sniff the ranges in the scent of wool and tar;
And it takes him back in fancy, half in laughter, half in tears,

To a sound of the other voices and a thought of the other years,
When the woolshed rand with bustle from the dawning of the day,
And the shear blades were a-clicking to the cry of 'wool away!'
When his face was somewhat browner and his frame was firmer set,
And he feels his flabby muscles with a feeling of regret.
Then the wool team slowly passes and his eyes go sadly back
To the dusty little table and the papers in the rack,
And his thoughts go to the terrace where his sickly children squall,
And he thinks there's something healthy in the bush life after all.

But we'll go no more a-droving in the wind or in the sun,
For our fathers' hearts have failed us and the droving days are done.
There's a nasty dash of danger where the long-horned bullock wheels,
And we like to live in comfort and to get our reg'lar meals.
And to hang about the townships suits us better, you'll agree,
For a job at washing bottles is the job for such as we.
Let us herd into the cities, let us crush and crowd and push
Till we lose the love of roving and we learn to hate the bush;
And we'll turn our aspirations to a city life and beer,
And we'll sneak across to England – it's a nicer place than here;
For there's not much risk of hardship where all comforts are in store,
And the theatres are plenty and the pubs are more and more.

But that ends it, Mister Lawson, and it's time to say good-bye,
We must agree to differ in all friendship, you and I;
And our personal opinions – well, they're scarcely worth a rush,
For there's some that like the city and there's some that like the bush;
And there's no one quite contented, as I've always heard it said,
Except one favoured person, and *he* turned out to be dead.
So we'll work our own salvation with the stoutest hearts we may,
And if fortune only favours we will take the road some day,
And go droving down the river 'neath the sunshine and the stars,
And then we'll come to Sydney and vermilionise the bars.

*(1892)*

## *A Bush Christening*

In the outer Barcoo where the churches are few,
  And men of religion are scanty,
On a road never cross'd 'cept by folk that are lost,
  One Michael Magee had a shanty.

Now this Mike was the dad of a ten-year-old lad,
  Plump, healthy, and stoutly conditioned;
He was strong as the best, but poor Mike had no rest
  For the youngster had never been christened.

And his wife used to cry, 'If the darlin' should die
  Saint Peter would not recognise him.'
But by luck he survived till a preacher arrived,
  Who agreed straightaway to baptise him.

Now the artful young rogue, while they held their collogue,
  With his ear to the keyhole was listenin',
And he muttered in fright while his features turned white,
  'What the divil and all is this christenin'?'

He was none of your dolts, he had seen them brand colts,
  And it seemed to his small understanding,
If the man in the frock made him one of the flock,
  It must mean something very like branding.

So away with a rush he set off for the bush,
  While the tears in his eyelids they glistened –
''Tis outrageous,' says he, 'to brand youngsters like me,
  I'll be dashed if I'll stop to be christened!'

Like a young native dog he ran into a log,
  And his father with language uncivil,
Never heeding the 'praste' cried aloud in his haste,
  'Come out and be christened, you divil!'

But he lay there as snug as a bug in a rug,
  And his parents in vain might reprove him,
Till his reverence spoke (he was fond of a joke)
  'I've a notion,' says he, 'that'll move him.'

'Poke a stick up the log, give the spalpeen a prog;
  Poke him aisy – don't hurt him or maim him,
'Tis not long that he'll stand, I've the water at hand,
  As he rushes out this end I'll name him.

'Here he comes, and for shame! ye've forgotten the name –
  Is it Patsy or Michael or Dinnis?'
Here the youngster ran out, and the priest gave a shout –
  'Take your chance, anyhow, wid "Maginnis"!'

As the howling young cub ran away to the scrub
  Where he knew that pursuit would be risky,
The priest, as he fled, flung a flask at his head
  That was labelled 'Maginnis's Whisky!'

And Maginnis Magee has been made a J.P.,
  And the one thing he hates more than sin is
To be asked by the folk who have heard of the joke,
  How he came to be christened 'Maginnis'!

*(1893)*

## *Black Swans*

As I lie at rest on a patch of clover
In the western park when the day is done,
I watch as the wild black swans fly over
With their phalanx turned to the sinking sun;
And I hear the clang of their leader crying
To a lagging mate in the rearward flying,
And they fade away in the darkness dying,
Where the stars are mustering one by one.

Oh! ye wild black swans, 'twere a world of wonder
For a while to join in your westward flight,
With the stars above and the dim earth under,
Through the cooling air of the glorious night.
As we swept along on our pinions winging,
We should catch the chime of a church-bell ringing,
Or the distant note of a torrent singing,
Or the far-off flash of a station light.

From the northern lakes with the reeds and rushes,
Where the hills are clothed with a purple haze,
Where the bellbirds chime and the songs of thrushes
Make music sweet in the jungle maze,
They will hold their course to the westward ever,
Till they reach the banks of the old grey river,
Where the waters wash, and the reed beds quiver
In the burning heat of the summer days.

Oh! ye strange wild birds, will ye bear a greeting
To the folk that live in that western land?
Then for every sweep of your pinions beating,
Ye shall bear a wish to the sunburnt band,
To the stalwart men who are stoutly fighting
With the heat and drought and dust storm smiting,
Yet whose life somehow has a strange inviting,
When once to the work they have put their hand.

Facing it yet! Oh, my friend stout-hearted,
What does it matter for rain or shine,
For the hopes deferred and the gain departed?
Nothing could conquer that heart of thine.
And thy health and strength are beyond confessing
As the only joys that are worth possessing.
May the days to come be as rich in blessing
As the days we spent in the auld lang syne.

I would fain go back to the old grey river,
To the old bush days when our hearts were light,
But, alas! those days they have fled for ever,
They are like the swans that have swept from sight.
And I know full well that the strangers' faces
Would meet us now in our dearest places;
For our day is dead and has left no traces
But the thoughts that live in my mind tonight.

There are folk long dead, and our hearts would sicken –
We would grieve for them with a bitter pain,
If the past could live and the dead could quicken,
We then might turn to that life again.
But on lonely nights we would hear them calling,
We should hear their steps on the pathways falling,
We should loathe the life with a hate appalling
In our lonely ridges by the ridge and plain.

In the silent park is a scent of clover,
And the distant roar of the town is dead,
And I hear once more as the swans fly over
Their far-off clamour from overhead.
They are flying west by their instinct guided,
And for man likewise is his fate decided,
And griefs apportioned and joys divided
By a mighty power with a purpose dread.

*(1893)*

# How Gilbert Died

There's never a stone at the sleeper's head,
  There's never a fence beside,
And the wandering stock on the grave may tread
  Unnoticed and undenied,
But the smallest child on the Watershed
  Can tell you how Gilbert died.

For he rode at dusk, with his comrade Dunn
  To the hut at the Stockman's Ford,
In the waning light of the sinking sun
  They peered with a fierce accord.
They were outlaws both – and on each man's head
  Was a thousand pounds reward.

They had taken toll of the country round,
  And the troopers came behind
With a black that tracked like a human hound
  In the scrub and the ranges blind:
He could run the trail where a white man's eye
  No sign of track could find.

He had hunted them out of the One Tree Hill
  And over the Old Man Plain,
But they wheeled their tracks with a wild beast's skill,
  And they made for the range again.
Then away to the hut where their grandsire dwelt,
  They rode with a loosened rein.

And their grandsire gave them a greeting bold:
  'Come in and rest in peace,
No safer place does the country hold –
  With the night pursuit must cease,
And we'll drink success to the roving boys,
  And to hell with the black police.'

But they went to death when the entered there,
  In the hut at the Stockman's Ford,
For their grandsire's words were as false as fair –
  They were doomed to the hangman's cord.
He had sold them both to the black police
  For the sake of the big reward.

In the depth of night there are forms that glide
  As stealthy as serpents creep,
And around the hut where the outlaws hide
  They plant in the shadows deep,
And they wait till the first faint flush of dawn
  Shall awaken their prey from sleep.

But Gilbert wakes while night is dark –
  A restless sleeper, aye,
He has heard the sound of a sheepdog's bark,
  And his horse's warning neigh,
And he says to his mate, 'There are hawks abroad,
  And it's time that we went away.'

Their rifles stood as the stretcher head
  Their bridles lay to hand,
They wakened the old man out of his bed,
  When they heard the sharp command:
'In the name of the Queen lay down your arms,
  Now, Dunn and Gilbert, stand!'

Then Gilbert reached for his rifle true
  That close at his hand he kept,
He pointed it straight at the voice and drew,
  But never a flash outleapt,
For the water ran from the rifle breach –
  It was drenched while the outlaws slept.

Then he dropped the piece with a bitter oath,
  And he turned to his comrade Dunn:
'We are sold,' he said, 'we are dead men both,
  But there may be a chance for one;
I'll stop and I'll fight with the pistol here,
  You take to your heels and run.'

So Dunn crept out on his hands and knees
  In the dim, half-dawning light,
And he made his way to a patch of trees,
  And vanished among the night,
And the trackers hunted his tracks all day,
  But they never could trace his flight.

But Gilbert walked from the open door
  In a confident style and rash;
He heard at his side the rifle roar,
  And he heard the bullets crash.
But he laughed as he lifted his pistol-hand,
  And he fired at the rifle flash.

Then out of the shadows the troopers aimed
  At his voice and the pistol sound,
With the rifle flashes the darkness flames,
  He staggered and spun around,
And they riddled his body with rifle balls
  As it lay on the blood-soaked ground.

There's never a stone at the sleeper's head
  There's never a fence beside,
And the wandering stock on the grave may tread
  Unnoticed and undenied,
But the smallest child on the Watershed
  Can tell you how Gilbert died.

*(1894)*

# *The Man Who Was Away*

The widow sought the lawyer's room with children three in tow,
She told the lawyer her tale in tones of deepest woe.
Said she, 'My husband took to drink for pains in his inside,
And never drew a sober breath from then until he died.

'He never drew a sober breath, he died without a will,
And I must sell the bit of land the childer's mouths to fill.
There's some is grown and gone away, but some is childer yet,
And times is very bad indeed – a livin's hard to get.

'There's Min and Sis and little Chris, they stops at home with me,
And Sal has married Greenhide Bill that breaks for Bingeree.
And Fred is drovin' Conroy's sheep along the Castlereagh,
And Charley's shearin' down the Bland, and Peter is away.'

The lawyer wrote the details down in the ink of legal blue –
'There's Minnie, Susan, Christopher, they stop at home with you;
There's Sarah, Frederick and Charles, I'll write to them to-day,
But what about the other one – the one who is away?

'You'll have to furnish his consent to sell the bit of land.'
The widow shuffled in her seat, 'Oh, don't you understand?
I thought a lawyer ought to know – I don't know what to say –
You'll have to do without him, boss, for Peter is away.'

But here the little boy spoke up – said he, 'We thought you knew;
He's done six months in Goulburn gaol – he's got six more to do.'
Thus in one comprehensive flash he made it clear as day,
The mystery of Peter's life – the man who was away.

*(1894)*

## *Saltbush Bill*

Now this is the law of the Overland that all in the west obey,
A man must cover with travelling sheep a six-mile stage a day;
But this is the law which the drovers make, right easily understood,
They travel their stage where the grass is bad, but they camp where
 the grass is good;
They camp, and they ravage the squatter's grass till never a blade
 remains,
Then they drift away as white clouds drift on the edge of the
 saltbush plains,
From camp to camp and from run to run they battle it hand to
 hand,
For a blade of grass and the right to pass on the track of the
 Overland.

For this is the law of the Great Stock Routes, 'tis written in white
 and black –
The man that goes with a travelling mob must keep to a half-mile
 track;
And the drovers keep to a half-mile track on the runs where the
 grass is dead,
But they spread their sheep on a well-grassed run till they go with
 a two-mile spread.
So the squatters hurry the drovers on from dawn till the fall of
 night,
And the squatters' dogs and the drovers' dogs get mixed in a
 deadly fight;
Yet the squatters' men, though they hunt the mob, are willing the
 peace to keep,
For the drovers learn how to use their hands when they go with
 the travelling sheep;
But this is the tale of a Jackaroo that came from a foreign strand,
And the fight that he fought with Saltbush Bill, the King of the
 Overland.

Now Saltbush Bill was a drover tough, as ever the country knew,
He had fought his way on the Great Stock Routes from the sea to the
Big Barcoo;
He could tell when he came to a friendly run that gave him a chance
to spread,
And he knew where the hungry owners were that hurried his sheep
ahead;
He was drifting down in the Eighty drought with a mob that could
scarcely creep,
(When the kangaroos by the thousands starve, it is rough on the
travelling sheep.)
And he camped one night at the crossing place on the edge of the
Wilga run,
'We must manage a feed for them here,' he said, 'or the half of the
mob are done!'
So he spread them out when they left the camp wherever they liked
to go,
Till he grew aware of a Jackaroo with station men in tow.
And they set to work on the straggling sheep, and with many a
stockwhip crack
They forced them in where the grass was dead in the space of the
half-mile track;
So William prayed that the hand of fate might suddenly strike him
blue
But he'd get some grass for his starving sheep in the teeth of that
Jackaroo.

So he turned and he cursed the Jackaroo, he cursed him alive or dead,
From the soles of his great unwieldy feet to the crown of his ugly head,
With an extra curse on the moke he rode and the cur at his heels that
ran,
Till the Jackaroo from his horse got down and he went for the drover man;
With the station hand for his picker-up, though the sheep ran loose
the while,
The battled it out on the saltbush plain in the regular prize ring style.

Now, the new chum fought for his honour's sake and the pride of the
English race,
But the drover fought for his daily bread with a smile on his bearded
face;
So he shifted ground and he sparred for wind and he made it a
lengthy mill,
And from time to time as his scouts came in they whispered to
Saltbush Bill –
'We have spread the sheep with a two-mile spread, and the grass it is
something grand,
You must stick to him, Bill, for another round for the pride of the
Overland.'

The new chum made it a rushing fight, though never a blow got home,
Till the sun rode high in the cloudless sky and glared on the brick-red
loam,
Till the sheep drew in to the shelter trees and settled them down to rest,
Then the drover said he would fight no more and he gave his
opponent best.
So the new chum rode to the homestead straight and he told them a
story grand
Of the desperate fight that he fought that day with the King of the
Overland.

And the tale went home to the public schools of the pluck of the
English swell,
How the drover fought for his very life, but blood in the end must tell.
But the travelling sheep and the Wilga sheep were boxed on the Old
Man Plain.
'Twas a full week's work ere they drafted out and hunted them off again,
With a week's good grass in their wretched hides, with a curse and a
stockwhip crack,
They hunted them off on the road once more to starve on the half-
mile track.
And Saltbush Bill, on the Overland, will many a time recite
How the best day's work that ever he did was the day that he lost the
fight.

*(1894)*

## *The Two Devines*

It was shearing time at the Myall Lake,
  And there rose the sound thro' the livelong day
Of the constant clash that the shear blades make
  When the fastest shearers are making play,
But there wasn't a man in the shearer's lines
That could shear a sheep with the two Devines.

They had rung the sheds of the east and west,
  Had beaten the cracks of the Walgett side,
And the Cooma shearers had giv'n them best –
  When they saw them shear, they were satisfied.
From the southern slopes to the western pines
They were noted men, were the two Devines.

'Twas a wether flock that had come to hand,
  Great struggling brutes, that the shearers shirk,
For the fleece was filled with the grass and sand,
  And seventy sheep was a big day's work.
'At a pound a hundred it's dashed hard lines
To shear such sheep,' said the two Devines.

But the shearers knew that they'd make a cheque
  When they came to deal with the station ewes;
They were bare of belly and bare of neck
  With a fleece as light as a kangaroo's.
'We will show the boss how a shear blade shines
When we reach those ewes,' said the two Devines.

But it chanced next day when the stunted pines
  Were swayed and stirred with the dawn wind's breath,
That a message came for the two Devines
  That their father lay at the point of death.
So away at speed through the whispering pines
Down the bridle track rode the two Devines.

It was fifty miles to their father's hut,
  And the dawn was bright when they rode away;
At the fall of night when the shed was shut
  And the men had rest from the toilsome day,
To the shed once more through the dark'ning pines
On their weary steeds came the two Devines.

'Well, you're back right sudden,' the super. said;
  'Is the old man dead and the funeral done?'
'Well, no, sir, he ain't not exactly dead,
  But as good as dead,' said the eldest son –
'And we couldn't bear such a chance to lose,
So we came straight back to tackle the ewes.'

They are shearing ewes at the Myall Lake,
  And the shed is merry the livelong day
With the clashing sound that the shear blades make
  When the fastest shearers are making play,
And a couple of 'hundred and ninety-nines'
Are tallies made by the two Devines.

*(1894)*

# *The Daylight is Dying*

The daylight is dying
  Away in the west,
The wild birds are flying
  In silence to rest;
In leafage and frondage
  Where shadows are deep,
They pass to its bondage –
  The kingdom of sleep.
And watched in their sleeping
  By stars in the height,
They rest in your keeping,
  Oh, wonderful night.

When night doth her glories
  Of starshine unfold,
'Tis then that the stories
  Of bushland are told.
Unnumbered I hold them
  In memories bright,
But who could unfold them,
  Or read them aright?
Beyond all denials
  The stars in their glories
The breeze in the myalls
  Are part of these stories.
The waving of grasses,
  The song of the river
That sings as it passes
  For ever and ever,
The hobble chains rattle,
  The calling of birds,
The lowing of cattle
  Must blend with the words.
Without these, indeed, you
  Would find it ere long,

As though I should read you
  The words of a song
That lamely would linger
  When lacking the rune,
The voice of the singer,
  The lilt of the tune.

But, as one half-hearing
  An old-time refrain,
With memory clearing,
  Recalls it again,
These tales, roughly wrought of
  The bush and its ways,
May call back a thought of
  The wandering days,
And, blending with each
  In the mem'ries that throng,
There haply shall reach
  You some echo of song.

*(1895)*

# *Jim Carew*

Born of a thoroughbred English race,
  Well proportioned and closely knit,
Neat of figure and handsome face,
  Always ready and always fit,
Hard and wiry of limb and thew,
That was the ne'er-do-well Jim Carew.

One of the sons of the good old land –
  Many a year since his like was known;
Never a game but he took command,
  Never a sport but he held his own;
Gained at his college a triple blue –
Good as they make them was Jim Carew.

Came to grief – was it card or horse?
  Nobody asked and nobody cared;
Ship him away to the bush of course,
  Ne'er-do-well fellows are easily spared;
Only of women a tolerable few
Sorrowed at parting with Jim Carew.

Gentleman Jim on the cattle camp,
  Sitting his horse with an easy grace;
But the reckless living has left its stamp
  In the deep drawn lines of that handsome face,
And a harder look in those eyes of blue:
Prompt at a quarrel is Jim Carew.

Billy the Lasher was out for gore –
  Twelve-stone navvy with chest of hair,
When he opened out with a hungry roar
  On a ten-stone man it was hardly fair;
But his wife was wise if his face she knew
By the time you were done with him, Jim Carew.

Gentleman Jim in the stockmen's hut
  Works with them, toils with them, side by side;
As to his past – well, his lips are shut.
  'Gentleman once,' say his mates with pride;
And the wildest Cornstalk can ne'er outdo
In feats of recklessness, Jim Carew.

What should he live for? A dull despair!
  Drink is his master and drags him down,
Water of Lethe that drowns all care.
  Gentleman Jim has a lot to drown,
And he reigns as king with a drunken crew,
Sinking to misery, Jim Carew.

Such is the end of the ne'er-do-well –
  Jimmy the Boozer, all down at heel;
But he straightens up when he's asked to tell
  His name and race, and a flash of steel
Still lightens up those eyes of blue –
'I am, or – no, I *was*, – Jim Carew.'

*(1895)*

# The Swagman's Rest

We buried old Bob where the bloodwoods wave
  At the foot of the Eaglehawk;
We fashioned a cross on the old man's grave,
  For fear that his ghost might walk;
We carved his name on a bloodwood tree,
  With the date of his sad decease,
And in place of 'Died from effects of spree',
  We wrote, 'May he rest in peace'.

For Bob was known on the Overland,
  A regular old bush wag,
Tramping along in the dust and sand,
  Humping his well worn swag.
He would camp for days in the river bed,
  And loiter and 'fish for whales'.
'I'm into the swagman's yard,' he said,
  'And I never shall find the rails.'

But he found the rails on that summer night
  For a better place – or worse,
As we watched by turns in the flickering light
  With an old black gin for nurse.
The breeze came in with the scent of pine,
  The river sounded clear,
When a change came on, and we saw the sign
  That told us the end was near.

But he spoke in a cultured voice and low –
  'I fancy they've "sent the route";
I once was an army man, you know,
  Though now I'm a drunken brute;
But bury me out where the bloodwoods wave,
  And if ever you're fairly stuck,
Just take and shovel me out of the grave,
  And, maybe, I'll bring you luck.

'For I've always heard –' here his voice fell weak,
His strength was well-nigh sped,
He gasped and struggled and tried to speak,
Then fell in a moment – dead.
Thus ended a wasted life and hard,
Of energies misapplied –
Old Bob was out of the 'swagman's yard'
And over the Great Divide.

The drought came down on the field and flock,
And never a raindrop fell,
Though the tortured moans of the starving stock
Might soften a fiend from hell.
And we thought of the hint that the swagman gave
When he went to the Great Unseen –
We shovelled the skeleton out of the grave
To see what his hint might mean.

We dug where the cross and the graveposts were,
We shovelled away the mould,
When sudden a vein of quartz lay bare
All gleaming with yellow gold.
'Twas a reef with never a fault nor baulk
Than ran from the range's crest,
And the richest mine on the Eaglehawk
Is known as 'The Swagman's Rest'.

*(1895)*

# *The Wind's Message*

There came a whisper down the Bland between the dawn and dark,
Above the tossing of the pines, above the river's flow;
It stirred the boughs of giant gums and stalwart ironbark;
It drifted where the wild ducks played amid the swamps below;
It brought a breath of mountain air from off the hills of pine,
A scent of eucalyptus trees in honey-laden bloom;
And drifting, drifting far away along the southern line
It caught from leaf and grass and fern a subtle strange perfume.

It reached the toiling city folk, but few there were that heard –
The rattle of their busy life had choked the whisper down;
And some but caught a fresh-blown breeze with scent of pine that stirred
A thought of blue hills far away beyond the smoky town;
And others heard the whisper pass, but could not understand
The magic of the breeze's breath that set their hearts aglow,
Nor how the roving wind could bring across the Overland
A sound of voices silent now and songs of long ago.

But some that heard the whisper clear were filled with vague unrest;
The breeze had brought its message home, they could not fixed abide;
Their fancies wandered all the day towards the blue hills' breast,
Towards the sunny slopes that lie along the riverside,
The mighty rolling western plains are very fair to see,
Where waving to the passing breeze the silver myalls stand,
But fairer are the giant hills, all rugged though they be,
From which the two great rivers rise that run along the Bland.

Oh! rocky range and rugged spur and river running clear,
That swings around the sudden bends with swirl of snow-white foam.
Though we, your sons, are far away, we sometimes seem to hear
The message that the breezes bring to call the wanderers home.
The mountain peaks are white with snow that feeds a thousand rills,
Along the river banks the maize grows tall on virgin land,
And we shall live to see once more those sunny southern hills,
And strike once more the bridle track that leads along the Bland.

*(1895)*

# *Under the Shadow of Kiley's Hill*

This is the place where they all were bred;
  Some of the rafters are standing still;
Now they are scattered and lost and dead,
Every one from the old nest fled,
  Out of the shadow of Kiley's Hill.

Better it is that they ne'er came back –
  Changes and chances are quickly rung;
Now the old homestead is gone to rack,
Green is the grass on the well-worn track
  Down by the gate where the roses clung.

Gone is the garden they kept with care;
  Left to decay at its own sweet will,
Fruit trees and flower beds eaten bare,
Cattle and sheep where the roses were,
  Under the shadow of Kiley's Hill.

Where are the children that throve and grew
  In the old homestead in days gone by?
One is away on the far Barcoo
Watching his cattle the long year through,
  Watching them starve in the droughts and die.

One in the town where all cares are rife,
  Weary with troubles that cramp and kill,
Fain would be done with the restless strife,
Fain would go back to the old bush life,
  Back to the shadow of Kiley's Hill.

One is away on the roving quest,
  Seeking his share of golden spoil,
Out in the wastes of the trackless west,
Wandering ever he gives the best
  Of his years and strength to the hopeless toil.

What of parents? That unkempt mound
  Shows where they slumber united still;
Rough is their grave, but they sleep as sound
Out on the range as on holy ground,
  Under the shadow of Kiley's Hill.

*(1895)*

# *Waltzing Matilda*

*Carrying a Swag*
*(Original Version)*

Oh there once was a swagman camped in the billabongs,
  Under the shade of a Coolibah tree;
And he sang as he looked at the old billy boiling,
  'Who'll come a-waltzing Matilda with me.'

Who'll come a-waltzing Matilda, my darling,
  Who'll come a-waltzing Matilda with me.
Waltzing Matilda and leading a water-bag,
  Who'll come a-waltzing Matilda with me.

Up came the jumbuck to drink at the waterhole,
  Up jumped the swagman and grabbed him in glee;
And he sang as he put him away in his tucker-bag,
  'You'll come a-waltzing Matilda with me.'

Who'll come a-waltzing Matilda, my darling,
  Who'll come a-waltzing Matilda with me.
Waltzing Matilda and leading a water-bag,
  Who'll come a-waltzing Matilda with me.

Up came the squatter a-riding his thoroughbred;
  Up came policemen – one, two, and three.
'Whose is the jumbuck you've got in the tucker-bag?
  You'll come a-waltzing Matilda with me.'

Who'll come a-waltzing Matilda, my darling,
  Who'll come a-waltzing Matilda with me.
Waltzing Matilda and leading a water-bag,
  Who'll come a-waltzing Matilda with me.

Up sprang the swagman and jumped in the waterhole,
  Drowning himself by the Coolibah tree;
And his voice may be heard as it sings in the billabongs,
  'Who'll come a-waltzing Matilda with me.'

Who'll come a-waltzing Matilda, my darling,
  Who'll come a-waltzing Matilda with me.
Waltzing Matilda and leading a water-bag,
  Who'll come a-waltzing Matilda with me.

*(1903: written 1895)*

## *Waltzing Matilda*

*(Popular Version)*

Once a jolly swagman camped by a billabong
  Under the shade of a coolibah tree,
And he sang as he watched and waited till his billy boiled,
  Who'll come a-waltzing Matilda with me?

*Chorus*
Waltzing Matilda, waltzing Matilda,
  Who'll come a-waltzing Matilda with me?
And he sang as he watched and waited till his billy boiled,
  Who'll come a-waltzing Matilda with me?

Down came a jumbuck to drink at that billabong,
  Up jumped the swagman and grabbed him with glee,
And he sang as he shoved that jumbuck in his tucker-bag,
  You'll come a-waltzing Matilda with me!

Waltzing Matilda, waltzing Matilda,
  You'll come a-waltzing Matilda with me!
And he sang as he shoved that jumbuck in his tucker-bag,
  You'll come a-waltzing Matilda with me!

Up rode the squatter mounted on his thoroughbred,
  Down came the troopers, one, two, three,
Whose that jolly jumbuck you've got in your tucker-bag,
  You'll come a-waltzing Matilda with me!

Waltzing Matilda, waltzing Matilda,
  You'll come a-waltzing Matilda with me!
Whose that jolly jumbuck you've got in your tucker-bag,
  You'll come a-waltzing Matilda with me!

Up jumped the swagman and sprang into the billabong,
  You'll never catch me alive, said he,
And his ghost may be heard as you pass by that billabong,
  You'll come a-waltzing Matilda with me!

Waltzing Matilda, waltzing Matilda,
  You'll never catch me alive, said he,
And his ghost may be heard as you pass by that billabong,
  You'll come a-waltzing Matilda with me!

# *Brumby's Run*

*The Aboriginal term for a wild horse is 'brumby'. At a recent trial in Sydney a supreme court judge, hearing of 'brumby horses', asked, 'who is Brumby, and where is his run?'*

It lies beyond the Western Pines
  Towards the sinking sun,
And not a survey mark defines
  The bounds of 'Brumby's Run'.

On odds and ends of mountain land
  On tracks of range and rock,
Where no one else can make a stand,
  Old Brumby rears his stock –

A wild, unhandled lot they are
  Of every shape and breed,
They venture out 'neath moon and star
  Along the flats to feed.

But when the dawn makes pink the sky
  And steals along the plain,
The Brumby horses turn and fly
  Towards the hills again.

The traveller by the mountain track
  May hear their hoofbeats pass,
And catch a glimpse of brown and black,
  Dim shadows on the grass.

The eager stock horse pricks his ears
  And lifts his head on high
In wild excitement when he hears
  The Brumby mob go by.

Old Brumby asks no price or fee
  O'er all his wild domains:
The man who yards his stock is free
  To keep them for his pains.

So, off to scour the mountainside
  With eager eyes aglow,
To strongholds where the wild mobs hide
  The gully-rakers go.

A rush of horses through the trees,
  A red shirt making play;
A sound of stockwhips on the breeze,
  They vanish far away!

Ah, me! before our day is done
  We long with bitter pain
To ride once more on Brumby's run
  And yard his mob again.

*(1895)*

## *With the Cattle*

The drought is down on field and flock,
  The river bed is dry;
And we shift the starving stock
  Before the cattle die.
We muster up with weary hearts
  At breaking of the day,
And turn our heads to foreign parts,
  To take the stock away.
    And it's hunt 'em up and dog 'em,
    And it's get the whip and flog 'em,
For it's weary work is droving when they're dying every day;
    By stock routes bare and eaten,
    On dusty roads and beaten,
With half a chance to save their lives we take the stock away.

We cannot use the whip for shame
  On beasts that crawl along;
We have to drop the weak and lame,
  And try to save the strong;
The wrath of God is on the track,
  The drought fiend holds his sway,
With blows and cries and stockwhip crack
  We take the stock away.
    As they fall we leave them lying,
    With the crows to watch them dying,
Grim sextons of the Overland that fasten on their prey;
    By the fiery dust storm drifting,
    And the mocking mirage shifting,
In heat and drought and hopeless pain we take the stock away.

In dull despair the days go by
  With never hope of change,
But every stage we draw more nigh
  Towards the mountain range;

And some may live to climb the pass,
  And reach the great plateau,
And revel in the mountain grass,
  By streamlets fed with snow.
    As the mountain wind is blowing
    It starts the cattle lowing,
And calling to each other down the dusty long array;
    And there speaks a grizzled drover:
    'Well, thank God, the worst is over,
The creatures smell the mountain grass that's twenty miles away.'

They press towards the mountain grass,
  They look with eager eyes
Along the rugged stony pass,
  That slopes towards the skies;
Their feet may bleed from rocks and stones,
  But though the blood-drop starts,
They struggle on with stifled groans,
  For hope is in their hearts.
    And the cattle that are leading,
    Though their feet are worn and bleeding,
Are breaking to a kind of run – pull up, and let them go!
    For the mountain wind is blowing,
    And the mountain grass is growing,
They settle down by running streams ice-cold with melted snow.

The days are done of heat and drought
  Upon the stricken plain;
The wind has shifted right about,
  And brought the welcome rain;
The river runs with sullen roar,
  All flecked with yellow foam,
And we must take the road once more,
  To bring the cattle home.
    And it's 'Lads! we'll raise a chorus,
    There's a pleasant trip before us.'

And the horses bound beneath us as we start them down the track;
    And the drovers canter, singing,
    Through the sweet green grasses springing,
Towards the far-off mountain land, to bring the cattle back.

Are these the beasts we brought away
  That move so lively now?
They scatter off like flying spray
  Across the mountain's brow;
And dashing down the rugged range
  We hear the stockwhip crack,
Good faith, it is a welcome change
  To bring such cattle back.
    And it's 'Steady down the lead there!'
    And it's 'Let 'em stop and feed there!'
For they're wild as mountain eagles and their sides are all afoam;
    But they're settling down already,
    And they'll travel nice and steady,
With cheery call and jest and song we fetch the cattle home.

We have to watch them close at night
  For fear they'll make a rush,
And break away in headlong flight
  Across the open bush;
And by the campfire's cheery blaze,
  With mellow voice and strong,
We hear the lonely watchman raise
  The Overlander's song:
    'Oh! it's when we're done with roving,
    With the camping and the droving,
It's homeward down the Bland we'll go, and never more we'll roam;'
    While the stars shine out above us,
    Like the eyes of those who love us –
The eyes of those who watch and wait to greet the cattle home.

The plains are all awave with grass,
  The skies are deepest blue;
And leisurely the cattle pass
  And feed the long day through;
But when we sight the station gate,
  We make the stockwhips crack,
A welcome sound to those who wait
  To greet the cattle back:
    And through the twilight falling
    We hear their voices calling,
As the cattle splash across the ford and churn it into foam;
    And the children run to meet us,
    And our wives and sweethearts greet us,
Their heroes from the Overland who brought the cattle home.

*(1896)*

# Song of the Artesian Water

Now the stock have started dying, for the Lord has sent a drought;
But we're sick of prayers and Providence – we're going to do without;
With the derricks up above us and the solid earth below,
We are waiting at the lever for the word to let her to.
  Sinking down, deeper down,
  Oh, we'll sink it deeper down:
As the drill is plugging downward at a thousand feet of level,
If the Lord won't send us water, oh, we'll get it from the devil;
  Yes, we'll get it from the devil deeper down.

Now, our engine's built in Glasgow by a very canny Scot,
And he marked it twenty horsepower, but he don't know what is what:
When Canadian Bill is firing with the sun-dried gidgee logs,
She can equal thirty horses and a score or so of dogs.
  Sinking down, deeper down:
  Oh, we're going deeper down:
If we fail to get the water then it's ruin to the squatter,
For the drought is on the station and the weather's growing hotter,
  But we're bound to get the water deeper down.

But the shaft has started caving and the sinking's very slow,
And the yellow rods are bending in the water down below,
And the tubes are always jamming and they can't be made to shift
Till we nearly burst the engine with a forty horsepower lift.
  Sinking down, deeper down,
  Oh, we're going deeper down
Though the shaft is always caving, and the tubes are always jamming,
Yet we'll fight our way to water while the stubborn drill is ramming –
  While the stubborn drill is ramming deeper down.

But there's no artesian water, though we've passed three thousand feet,
And the contract price is growing and the boss is nearly beat.
But it must be down beneath us, and it's down we've got to go,
Though she's bumping on the solid rock four thousand feet below.
  Sinking down, deeper down,
  Oh, we're going deeper down:
And it's time they heard us knocking on the roof of Satan's dwellin';
But we'll get artesian water if we cave the roof of Hell in –
  Oh! We'll get artesian water deeper down.

But it's hark! the whistle's blowing with a wild, exultant blast,
And the boys are madly cheering, for they've struck the flow at last,
And it's rushing up the tubing from four thousand feet below
Till it spouts above the casing in a million-gallon flow.
  And it's down, deeper down –
  Oh, it comes from deeper down;
It is flowing, ever flowing, in a free, unstinted measure
From the silent hidden places where the old earth hides her treasure –
  Where the old earth hides her treasure deeper down.

And it's clear away the timber, and it's let the water run:
How it glimmers in the shadow, how it flashes in the sun!
By the silent belts of timber, by the miles of blazing plain
It is bringing hope and comfort to the thirsty land again.
  Flowing down, further down;
  It is flowing further down
To the tortured thirsty cattle, bringing gladness in its going;
Through the droughty days of summer it is flowing, ever flowing –
  It is flowing, ever flowing, further down.

*(1896)*

# *The Story of Mongrel Grey*

This is the story the stockman told,
  On the cattle camp, when the stars were bright;
The moon rose up like a globe of gold
  And flooded the plain with her mellow light.
We watched the cattle till dawn of day
And he told me the story of the Mongrel Grey.

'He was a knock-about station hack,
  Spurred and walloped, and banged and beat;
Ridden all day with a sore on his back,
  Left all night with nothing to eat.
That was a matter of everyday –
Common occurrence to Mongrel Grey.

'Pr'aps we'd have sold him, but someone heard
  He was bred out back on a flooded run,
Where he learnt to swim like a water bird,
  Midnight or midday were all as one.
In the flooded ground he could find his way,
Nothing could puzzle old Mongrel Grey.

''Tis a special gift that some horses learn,
  When the floods are out they will splash along
In girth-deep water, and twist and turn
  From hidden channel and billabong.
Never mistaking the road to go,
For a man may guess – but the horses *know.*

'I was camping out with my youngest son
  – Bit of a nipper just learnt to speak –
In an empty hut on the lower run,
  Shooting and fishing in Conroy's Creek.
The youngster toddled about all day,
And with our horses was Mongrel Grey.

'All of a sudden the flood came down
  Fresh from the hills with the mountain rain,
Roaring and eddying, rank and brown,
  Over the flats and across the plain.
Rising and falling – fall of night –
Nothing but water appeared in sight!

''Tis a nasty place when the floods are out,
  Even in daylight, for all around
Channels and billabongs twist about,
  Stretching for miles in the flooded ground.
And to move was a hopeless thing to try
In the dark, with the water just racing by.

'I had to try it, I heard a roar,
  And the wind swept down with the blinding rain;
And the water rose till it reached the floor
  Of our highest room, and 'twas very plain
The way the water was sweeping down
We must shift for the highlands at once, or drown.

'Off to the stable I splashed, and found
  The horses shaking with cold and fright;
I led them down to the lower ground,
  But never a yard would they swim that night!
They reared and snorted and turned away,
And none would face it but Mongrel Grey.

'I bound the child on the horse's back,
  And we started off with a prayer to Heaven,
Through the rain and the wind and the pitchy black,
  For I knew that the instinct God has given
To guide His creatures by night and day
Would lead the footsteps of Mongrel Grey.

'He struck deep water at once and swam –
  I swam beside him and held his mane –
Till we touched the bank of the broken dam
  In shallow water – then off again,
Swimming in darkness across the flood,
Rank with the smell of the drifting mud.

'He turned and twisted across and back,
  Choosing the places to wade or swim,
Picking the safest and shortest track,
  The pitchy darkness was clear to him.
Did he strike the crossing by sight or smell?
The Lord that led him alone could tell!

'He dodged the timber whene'er he could,
  But the timber brought us to grief at last;
I was partly stunned by a log of wood,
  That struck my head as it drifted past;
And I lost my grip of the brave old grey,
And in half a second he swept away.

'I reached a tree, where I had to stay,
  And did a perish for two days hard;
And lived on water – but Mongrel Grey,
  He walked right into the homestead yard
At dawn next morning, and grazed around,
With the child on top of him safe and sound.

'We keep him now for the wife to ride,
  Nothing too good for him now of course;
Never a whip on his fat old hide,
  For she owes the child to that old grey horse.
And not Old Tyson himself could pay,
The purchase money of Mongrel Grey.'

*(1896)*

# Pioneers

They came of bold and roving stock that would not fixed abide;
They were the sons of field and flock since e'er they learned to ride;
We may not hope to see such men in these degenerate years
As those explorers of the bush – the brave old pioneers.

'Twas they who rode the trackless bush in heat and storm and drought;
'Twas they that heard the master-word that called them further out;
'Twas they that followed up the trail the mountain cattle made,
And pressed across the mighty range where now their bones are laid.

But now the times are dull and slow, the brave old days are dead
When hardy bushmen started out, and forced their way ahead
By tangled scrub and forests grim towards the unknown west,
And spied the far-off promised land from off the range's crest.

Oh! ye, that sleep in lonely graves by distant ridge and plain,
We drink to you in silence now as Christmas comes again,
The men who fought the wilderness through rough unsettled years –
The founders of our nation's life, the brave old pioneers.

*(1896)*

THE
ER'S ARMS'
CHAMP.

# By the Grey Gulf-Water

Far to the northward there lies a land,
  A wonderful land that the winds blow over,
And none may fathom nor understand
  The charm it holds for the restless rover;
A great grey chaos – a land half made,
  Where endless space is and no life stirreth;
And the soul of a man will recoil afraid
  From the sphinx-like visage that Nature weareth.
But old Dame Nature, though scornful, craves
  Her dole of death and her share of slaughter;
Many indeed are the nameless graves
  Where her victims sleep by the Grey Gulf-water.

Slowly and slowly those grey streams glide,
  Drifting along with a languid motion,
Lapping the reed beds on either side,
  Wending their way to the Northern Ocean.
Grey are the plains where the emus pass
  Silent and slow, with their staid demeanour;
Over the dead men's graves the grass
  Maybe is waving a trifle greener.
Down in the world where men toil and spin
  Dame Nature smiles as man's hand has taught her;
Only the dead men her smiles can win
  In the great lone land by the Grey Gulf-water.

For the strength of man is an insect's strength,
  In the fate of that mighty plain and river,
And the life of a man is a moment's length
  To the life of the stream that will run for ever.
And so it cometh they take no part
  In small-world worries; each hardy rover
Rideth abroad and is light of heart,
  With the plains around and the blue sky over.
And up in the heavens the brown lark sings
  The songs that the strange wild land has taught her;
Full of thanksgiving her sweet song rings –
  And I wish I were back by the Grey Gulf-water.

*(1897)*

# *Saltbush Bill's Second Fight*

The news came down on the Castlereagh, and went to the world at large,
That twenty thousand travelling sheep, with Saltbush Bill in charge,
Were drifting down from a dried-out run to ravage the Castlereagh;
And the squatters swore when they heard the news, and wished they were well away:
For the name and the fame of Saltbush Bill were over the countryside
For the wonderful way he fed his sheep, and the dodges and tricks he tried.
He would lose his way on a Main Stock Route, and stray to the squatters' grass;
He would come to a run with the boss away, and swear he had leave to pass;
And back of all and behind it all, as well the squatters knew,
If he had to fight, he would fight all day, so long as his sheep got through:
But this is the story of Stingy Smith, the owner of Hard Times Hill,
And the way that he chanced on a fighting man to reckon with Saltbush Bill.

'Twas Stingy Smith on his stockyard sat, and prayed for an early spring,
When he stared at sight of a clean-shaved tramp, who walked with jaunty swing;
For a clean-shaved tramp with a jaunty walk a-swinging along the track
Is as rare a thing as a feathered frog on the desolate roads outback.
So the tramp he made for the travellers' hut, and asked could he camp the night;
But Stingy Smith had a bright idea, and he said to him, 'Can you fight?'
'Why, what's the game?' said the clean-shaved tramp, as he looked at him up and down –
'If you want a battle, get off that fence, and I'll kill you for half-a-crown!

But, Boss, you'd better not fight with me, it wouldn't be fair nor right;
I'm Stiffener Joe, from the Rocks Brigade, and I killed a man in a fight:
I served two years for it, fair and square, and now I'm a trampin'
back,
To look for a peaceful quiet life away on the outside track –'
'Oh, it's not myself, but a drover chap,' said Stingy Smith with glee;
'A bullying fellow, called Saltbush Bill – and you are the man for me.
He's on the road with his hungry sheep, and he's certain to raise a row,
For he's bullied the whole of the Castlereagh till he's got them under
cow –
Just pick a quarrel and raise a fight, and leather him good and hard,
And I'll take good care that his wretched sheep don't wander a half
a yard.
It's a five-pound job if you belt him well – do anything short of kill,
For there isn't a beak on the Castlereagh will fine you for Saltbush
Bill.'

'I'll take the job,' said the fighting man, 'and hot as this cove appears,
He'll stand no chance with a bloke like me, what's lived on the game
for years;
For he's maybe learnt in a boxing school, and sparred for a round
or so,
But I've fought all hands in a ten foot ring each night in a travelling
show;
They earnt a pound if they stayed three rounds, and they tried for it
every night –
In a ten foot ring! Oh, that's the game that teaches a bloke to fight,
For they'd rush and clinch, it was Dublin Rules, and we drew no
colour line;
And they all tried hard for to earn the pound, but they got no pound
of mine:
If I saw no chance in the opening round I'd slog at their wind, and
wait
Till an opening came – and it *always* came – and I settled 'em, sure
as fate;
Left on the ribs and right on the jaw – and, when the chance
comes, *make sure*!
And it's there a professional bloke like me gets home on an amateur:

'For it's my experience every day, and I make no doubt it's yours
That a third-class pro is an over-match for the best of the amateurs –'
'Oh, take your swag to the travellers' hut,' said Smith, 'for you waste
your breath;
You've a first-class chance, if you lose the fight, of talking your men
to death.
I'll tell the cook you're to have your grub, and see that you eat your
fill,
And come to the scratch all fit and well to leather this Saltbush Bill.'

'Twas Saltbush Bill, and his travelling sheep were wending their
weary way
On the Main Stock Route, through the Hard Times Run, on their
six-mile stage a day;
And he strayed a mile from the Main Stock Route, and started to
feed along,
And, when Stingy Smith came up, Bill said that the Route was
surveyed wrong;
And he tried to prove that the sheep had rushed and strayed from
their camp at night,
But the fighting man he kicked Bill's dog, and of course that meant
a fight:

So they sparred and fought, and they shifted ground and never a
sound was heard
But the thudding of fists on their brawny ribs, and the seconds'
muttered word,
Till the fighting man shot home his left on the ribs with a mighty
clout,
And his right flashed up with a half-arm blow – and Saltbush Bill
'went out'.
He fell face down, and towards the blow; and their hearts with fear
were filled,
For he lay as still as a fallen tree, and they thought that he must be
killed.

So Stingy Smith and the fighting man, they lifted him from the ground,
And sent to home for a brandy flask, and they slowly fetched him round;
But his head was bad, and his jaw was hurt – in fact, he could scarcely speak –
So they let him spell till he got his wits, and he camped on the run a week,
While the travelling sheep went here and there, wherever they liked to stray,
Till Saltbush Bill was fit once more for the track to the Castlereagh.

Then Stingy Smith he wrote a note, and gave to the fighting man:
'Twas writ to the boss of the neighbouring run, and thus the missive ran:
'The man with this is a fighting man, one Stiffener Joe by name;
He came near murdering Saltbush Bill, and I found it a costly game:
But it's worth your while to employ the chap, for there isn't the slightest doubt
You'll have no trouble from Saltbush Bill while this man hangs about –'
But an answer came by the next week's mail, with news that might well appal:
'The man you sent with a note is not a fighting man at all!
He has shaved his beard, and has cut his hair, but I spotted him at a look;
He is Tom Devine, who has worked for years for Saltbush Bill as cook.
Bill coached him up in the fighting yarn, and taught him the tale by rote,
And they shammed to fight, and they got your grass and divided your five-pound note.
'Twas a clean take-in, and you'll find it wise – 'twill save you a lot of pelf –
When next you're hiring a fighting man, just fight him a round yourself.'

And the teamsters out on the Castlereagh, when they meet with a
week of rain,
And the waggon sinks to its axle-tree, deep down in the black soil
plain,
When the bullocks wade in a sea of mud, and strain at the load of
wool,
And the cattle dogs at the bullocks' heels are biting to make them pull,
When the offside driver flays the team, and curses them while he
flogs,
And the air is thick with the language used, and the clamour of
men and dogs –
The teamsters say, as they pause to rest and moisten each hairy
throat,
They wish they could swear like Stingy Smith when he read that
neighbour's note.

*(1897)*

## *It's Grand*

It's grand to be a squatter
  And sit upon a post,
And watch your little ewes and lambs
  A-giving up the ghost.

It's grand to be a 'cockie'
  With wife and kids to keep,
And find an all-wise Providence
  Has mustered all your sheep.

It's grand to be a western man,
  With shovel in your hand,
To dig your little homestead out
  From underneath the sand.

It's grand to be a shearer,
  Along the Darling side,
And pluck the wool from the stinking sheep
  That some days since have died.

It's grand to be a rabbit
  And breed till all is blue,
And then to die in heaps because
  There's nothing left to chew.

It's grand to be a Minister
  And travel like a swell,
And tell the central district folk
  To go to – Inverell.

It's grand to be a Socialist
  And lead the bold array
That marches to prosperity
  At seven bob a day.

It's grand to be an unemployed
  And lie in the Domain,
And wake up every second day
  And go to sleep again.

It's grand to borrow English tin
  To pay for wharves and Rocks,
And then to find it isn't in
  The little money-box.

It's grand to be a democrat
  And toady to the mob,
For fear that if you told the truth
  They'd hunt you from your job.

It's grand to be a lot of things
  In this fair southern land,
But if the Lord would send us rain,
  That would, indeed, be grand!

*(1902)*

# *The Old Australian Ways*

The London lights are far abeam
  Behind a bank of cloud,
Along the shore the gaslights gleam,
  The gale is piping loud;
And down the Channel, groping blind,
  We drive her through the haze
Towards the land we left behind –
The good old land of 'never mind',
  And old Australian ways.

The narrow ways of English folk
  Are not for such as we;
They bear the long-accustomed yoke
  Of staid conservancy:
But all our roads are new and strange
  And through our blood there runs
The vagabonding love of change
That drove us westward of the range
  And westward of the suns.

The city folk go to and fro
  Behind a prison's bars,
They never feel the breezes blow
  And never see the stars;
They never hear in blossomed trees
  The music low and sweet
Of wild birds making melodies,
Nor catch the little laughing breeze
  That whispers in the wheat.

Our fathers came of roving stock
  That could not fixed abide:
And we have followed field and flock
  Since e'er we learnt to ride;
By miner's camp and shearing shed,
  In land of heat and drought,
We followed where our fortunes led,
With fortune always on ahead
  And always further out.

The wind is in the barley grass,
  The wattles are in bloom;
The breezes greet us as they pass
  With honey-sweet perfume;
The parakeets go screaming by
  With flash of golden wing,
And from the swamp the wild ducks cry
Their long-drawn note of revelry,
  Rejoicing at the spring.

So throw the weary pen aside
  And let the papers rest,
For we must saddle up and ride
  Towards the blue hill's breast;
And we must travel far and fast
  Across their rugged maze,
To find the Spring of Youth at last,
And call back from the buried past
  The old Australian ways.

When Clancy took the drover's track
  In years of long ago,
He drifted to the outer back
  Beyond the Overflow;
By rolling plain and rocky shelf,
  With stockwhip in his hand,
He reached at last, oh lucky elf,
The town of Come-and-Help-Yourself
  In Rough-and-Ready Land.

And if it be that you would know
  The tracks he used to ride,
Then you must saddle up and go
  Beyond the Queensland side –
Beyond the reach of rule or law,
  To ride the long day through,
In Nature's homestead – filled with awe,
You then might see what Clancy saw
  And know what Clancy knew.

*(1902)*

# The Road to Gundagai

The mountain road goes up and down,
From Gundagai to Tumut town.

And branching off there runs a track,
Across the foothills grim and black,

Across the plains and ranges grey
To Sydney city far away.

It came by chance one day that I
From Tumut rode to Gundagai,

And reached about the evening tide
The crossing where the roads divide;

And, waiting at the crossing place,
I saw a maiden fair of face,

With eyes of deepest violet blue,
And cheeks to match the rose in hue –

The fairest maids Australia knows
Are bred among the mountain snows.

Then, fearing I might go astray,
I asked if she could show the way.

Her voice might well a man bewitch –
Its tones so supple, deep, and rich.

'The tracks are clear,' she made reply,
'And this goes down to Sydney town,
And that one goes to Gundagai.'

Then slowly, looking coyly back,
She went along the Sydney track.

And I for one was well content
To go the road the lady went;

But round the turn a swain she met –
The kiss she gave him haunts me yet!

I turned and travelled with a sigh
The lonely road to Gundagai.

*(1902)*

## *Santa Claus in the Bush*

It chanced out back at the Christmas time,
  When the wheat was ripe and tall,
A stranger rode to the farmer's gate,
  A sturdy man, and a small.

'Run down, run down, my little son Jack,
  And bid the stranger stay;
And we'll hae a crack for the "Auld Lang Syne",
  For tomorrow is Christmas Day.'

'Nay now, nay now,' said the dour gude wife,
  'But ye should let him be;
He's maybe only a drover chap
  From the land o' the Darling Pea.

'Wi' a drover's tales, and a drover's thirst
  To swiggle the whole night through;
Or he's maybe a life assurance carle,
  To talk ye black and blue.'

'Gude wife, he's never a drover chap,
  For their swags are neat and thin;
And he's never a life assurance carle,
  Wi' the brick dust burnt in his skin.

'Gude wife, gude wife, be not so dour,
  For the wheat stands ripe and tall,
And we shore wi' a seven-pound fleece this year,
  Ewes and weaners and all.

'There is grass to spare, and the stock are fat,
  When they whiles are gaunt and thin,
And we owe a tithe to the travelling poor,
  So we must ask him in.

'You can set him a chair to the table side,
  And give him a bite to eat;
An omelette made of a new-laid egg,
  Or a tasty piece of meat.'

'But the native cats have taken the fowls,
  They have na' left a leg;
And he'll get no omelette here at all
  Till the emu lays an egg!'

'Run down, run down, my little son Jack,
  To where the emus bide,
Ye shall find the old hen on the nest,
  While the old cock sits beside.

'But speak them fair, and speak them soft,
  Lest they kick ye a fearsome jolt,
Ye can give them a feed of the half-inch nails,
  Or a rusty carriage bolt.'

So little son Jack ran blithely down,
  With the rusty nails in hand,
Till he came where the emus fluffed and scratched,
  By their nest in the open sand.

And there he has gathered the new-laid egg,
  Would feed three men or four,
And the emus came for the half-inch nails,
  Right up to the settler's door.

'A waste of food,' said the dour gude wife,
  As she took the egg, wi' a frown.
'But he gets no meat, unless ye run
  A paddymelon down.'

'Gae oot, gae oot, my little son Jack,
  Wi' your twa-three doggies small;
Gin ye come not back wi' a paddymelon,
  Then come not back at all.'

So little son Jack he raced and he ran,
  And he was bare o' the feet,
And soon he captured the paddymelon,
  Was gorged wi' the stolen wheat.

'Sit down, sit down, my bonny wee man,
  To the best that the house can do –
An omelette made of the emu egg
  And a paddymelon stew.'

''Tis well, 'tis well,' said the bonny wee man;
  'I have eaten the wide world's meat,
But the food that is given wi' a right good will
  Is the sweetest food to eat.

'But the night draws on to the Christmas Day
  And I must rise and go,
For I have a mighty way to ride
  To the land of the Esquimaux.

'And it's there I must load my sledges up
  With the reindeers four-in-hand,
That go to the north, south, east, and west,
  To every Christian land.'

'To the Esquimaux,' said the dour good wife,
  'Ye suit my husband well!
For when he gets up on his journey horse
  He's a bit of a liar himsel'.'

Then out wi' a laugh went the bonny wee man
  To his old horse grazing nigh,
And away like a meteor flash they went
  Far off to the northern sky.

When the children woke on the Christmas morn
  They chattered might and main –
Wi' a sword and gun for little son Jack,
  And a braw new doll for Jane,
And a packet o'nails for the twa emus;
  But the dour gude wife got nane.

*(1906)*

# Sunrise on the Coast

Grey dawn on the sandhills – the night wind has drifted
  All night from the rollers a scent of the sea;
With the dawn the grey fog his battalions has lifted,
  At the scent of the morning they scatter and flee.

Like mariners calling the roll of their number
  The sea fowl put out to the infinite deep.
And far overhead – sinking softly to slumber –
  Worn out by their watching, the stars fall asleep.

To eastward where resteth the dome of the skies on
  The sea line stirs softly the curtain of night;
And far from behind the enshrouded horizon
  Comes the voice of a God saying, 'Let there be light.'

And lo, there is light! Evanescent and tender,
  It glows ruby-red where 'twas now ashen grey;
And purple and scarlet and gold in it splendour –
  Behold, 'tis that marvel, the birth of a day!

*(1914)*

## *Song of the Wheat*

We have sung the song of the droving days,
  Of the march of the travelling sheep;
By silent stages and lonely ways
  Thin, white battalions creep.
But the man who now by the land would thrive
  Must his spurs to a ploughshare beat.
Is there ever a man in the world alive
  To sing the song of the Wheat!

It's west by south of the Great Divide
  The grim grey plains run out,
Where the old flock masters lived and died
  In a ceaseless fight with drought.
Weary with waiting and hope deferred
  They were ready to own defeat,
Till at last they heard the master-word
  And the master-word was Wheat.

Yarran and Myall and Box and Pine –
  'Twas axe and fire for all;
They scarce could tarry to blaze the line
  Or wait for the trees to fall,
Ere the team was yoked and the gates flung wide,
  And the dust of the horses' feet
Rose up like a pillar of smoke to guide
  The wonderful march of Wheat.

Furrow by furrow, and fold by fold,
  The soil is turned on the plain;
Better than silver and better than gold
  Is the surface-mine of the grain.
Better than cattle and better than sheep
  In the fight with the drought and heat.
For a streak of stubbornness wide and deep
  Lies hid in a grain of Wheat.

When the stock is swept by the hand of fate,
  Deep down in his bed of clay
The brave brown Wheat will lie and wait
  For the resurrection day:
Lie hid while the whole world thinks him dead;
  But the spring rain, soft and sweet,
Will over the steaming paddocks spread
  The first green flush of the Wheat.

Green and amber and gold it grows
  When the sun sinks late in the west
And the breeze sweeps over the rippling rows
  Where the quail and the skylark nest.
Mountain or river or shining star,
  There's never a sight can beat –
Away to the skyline stretching far –
  A sea of the ripening Wheat.

When the burning harvest sun sinks low,
  And the shadows stretch on the plain,
The roaring strippers come and go
  Like ships on a sea of grain;
Till the lurching, groaning waggons bear
  Their tale of the load complete.
Of the world's great work he has done his share
  Who has gathered a crop of wheat.

Princes and Potentates and Czars,
  They travel in regal state,
But old King Wheat has a thousand cars
  For his trip to the water-gate;
And his thousand streamships breast the tide
  And plough thro' the wind and sleet
To the lands where the teeming millions bide
  That say, 'Thank god for Wheat!'

*(1914)*

## *The Mountain Squatter*

Here in my mountain home,
  On rugged hills and steep,
I sit and watch you come,
  O Riverina Sheep!

You come from fertile plains
  Where saltbush (sometimes) grows,
And flats that (when it rains)
  Will blossom like the rose.

But when the summer sun
  Gleams down like burnished brass
You have to leave your run
  And hustle off for grass.

'Tis then that – forced to roam –
  You come to where I keep,
Here in my mountain home,
  A boarding-house for sheep.

Around me where I sit
  The wary wombat goes,
A beast of little wit
  But what he knows, he *knows*.

The very same remark
  Applies to me also,
I don't give out a spark,
  But what I know, I *know*.

My brains perhaps would show
  No convolutions deep;
But anyhow I know
  The way to handle sheep.

These Riverina cracks,
  They do not care to ride
The half-inch hanging tracks
  Along the mountain side.

Their horses shake with fear
  When loosened boulders go,
With leaps, like startled deer,
  Down to the gulfs below.

Their very dogs will shirk,
  And drop their tails in fright
When asked to go and work
  A mob that's out of sight.

My little collie pup
  Works silently and wide,
You'll see her climbing up
  Alomng the mountain side.

As silent as a fox
  You'll see her come and go
A shadow through the rocks
  Where ash and messmate grow.

Then, lost to sight and sound
  Behind some rugged steep,
She works her way around
  And gathers up the sheep.

And, working wide and shy,
  She holds them rounded up.
The cash ain't coined to buy
  That little collie pup.

And so I draw a screw
  For self and dog and keep
To boundary-ride for you,
  Oh Riverina Sheep!

And when the autumn rain
  Has made the herbage grow,
You travel off again,
  And glad – no doubt – to go!

But some are left behind
  Around the mountain's spread,
For those we cannot find
  We put them down as dead.

But when we say *adieu*
  And close the boarding job,
I always find a few
  Fresh earmarks in my mob.

So what with those I sell,
  And what with those I keep,
You pay me pretty well,
  Oh Riverina Sheep!

It's up to me to shout
  Before we say goodbye –
'Here's to a howlin' drought
  All west of Gundagai!'

*(1915)*

# The Gundaroo Bullock

Oh, there's some that breeds the Devon that's as solid as a stone,
And there's some that breeds the brindle which they call the
'Goulburn Roan';
But amongst the breeds of cattle there are very, very few
Like the hairy-whiskered bullock that they bred at Gundaroo.

Far away by Grabben Gullen, where the Murrumbidgee flows,
There's a block of broken countryside where no one ever goes;
For the banks have gripped the squatters, and the free selectors too,
And their stock are always stolen by the men of Gundaroo.

There came a low informer to the Grabben Gullen side,
And he said to Smith the squatter, 'You must saddle up and ride,
For your bullock's in the harness-cask of Morgan Donahoo –
He's the greatest cattle-stealer that abides in Gundaroo.'

Oh, ho!' said Smith, the owner of the Grabben Gullen run,
'I'll go and get the troopers by the sinking of the sun,
And down into his homestead tonight we'll take a ride,
With warrants to identify the carcase and the hide.'

That night rode down the troopers, the squatter at their head,
They rode into the homestead, and pulled Morgan out of bed.
'Now, show to us the carcase of the bullock that you slew –
The great marsupial bullock that you killed in Gundaroo.'

They peered into the harness-cask, and found it wasn't full,
But down among the brine they saw some flesh and bits of wool.
'What's this?' exclaimed the trooper – 'an infant, I declare,'
Said Morgan, ''Tis the carcase of an old man native bear.
I heard that ye were coming, so an old man bear I slew,
Just to give you kindly welcome to my home in Gundaroo.

'The times is something awful, as you can plainly see,
The banks have broke the squatters, and they've broke the likes of me;
We can't afford a bullock – such expense would never do –
So an old man bear for breakfast is a treat in Gundaroo.'

And along by Grabben Gullen where the rushing river flows,
In the block of broken country where there's no one ever goes,
On the Upper Murrumbidgee they're a hospitable crew,
But you mustn't ask for 'bullock' when you go to Gundaroo.

*(1917)*

# LIST OF PHOTOGRAPHS

*Pages 8–9;* Mustering on Woodstock Station, Townsville - *John Oxley Library, State Library of Queensland*

*Pages 36–37;* Drover's camp at Prospect Creek, Blue Mountains, New South Wales, 1919 - *John Oxley Library, State Library of Queensland*

*Pages 48–49;* Drovers and a herd of cattle, Queensland - *John Oxley Library, State Library of Queensland*

*Pages 62–63;* Man on horseback droving sheep, Queensland, ca. 1915 - *John Oxley Library, State Library of Queensland*

*Pages 76–77;* Mustering and branding at Riverleigh, Chinchilla, Queensland, 1932 - *John Oxley Library, State Library of Queensland*

*Pages 84–85;* Carpenter's Arms Hotel at Sandy Creek in the Beenleigh district, ca. 1872 - *John Oxley Library, State Library of Queensland*

*Pages 98–99;* Drover's camp at Hughenden, Queensland, ca. 1916 - *John Oxley Library, State Library of Queensland*

*Endpapers;* Wild horses running © Corbis